WHERE DO WE GO FROM HERE?

WHERE DO WE GO FROM HERE?

ERWIN W. LUTZER

MOODY PRESS
CHICAGO

ISBN: 0-8024-9399-8

1 3 5 7 9 10 8 6 4
Printed in the United States of America

It's gone.

Remember when Francis Schaeffer told us that some day we would wake up and find out that the America we once knew was gone? *That day is here.*

We have crossed an invisible line, and there are no signs that we are capable of turning back. Like a boat caught in the mighty torrent of the Niagara river, we are being swept along in a powerful cultural current that just might put us over the brink.

When should we have first noticed that our ship was headed for dangerous waters? Perhaps it was as far back as 1963 when the Supreme Court ruled that is was unconstitutional to pray in our public schools. Or maybe it was in 1973 when the infamous *Roe v. Wade* decision legalized abortion for any reason. These were two unmistakable signs that our ship of state was veering off course. Now the precarious stream we have chosen has become a river, and the river has become a flood.

Daily, perhaps hourly, we are losing the war for America's heart and mind. We must understand the direction and speed of this cultural river that has spilled over and engulfed our land. We must also ask, What should we be doing at this critical hour?

This booklet is above all a message of hope, a message intended *to help us refocus our priorities in a day of great opportunity.* Never before in American history has it been more important for the church to be all that it can be in a society that is increasingly hostile to Christian values. We have come to a crisis for which the church must be prepared.

Before I seek to give both hope and direction to the church at this time of uncertainty, we need to survey the extent of the moral and spiritual devastation we see around us. Let's look at where we *are* before we outline what we should *do.*

WHERE WE ARE AS A SOCIETY

Five battles that militant secularists appear to be winning concern our religious freedom, our schools, abortion, the media, and homosexual rights.

Freedom of Religion

Today the courts play an increasingly important role in the battle for America. Our founding fathers wrote,

"Congress shall make no law respecting the establishment of religion or prohibiting the free exercise thereof." This First Amendment, which was specifically intended to guarantee freedom of expression, is now being used to severely curb religious liberty.

When Roger Baldwin began the American Civil Liberties Union (ACLU) in 1925, he stated openly his belief that the First Amendment could be used to impose a liberal social agenda on the United States. (In 1935 he said, "Communism is the goal.") The courts, he believed, could be used to circumvent democracy. Through the judicial process, religious influence in education, government, and society could be severely restricted. How right he was!

Consider the ruling of a federal appeals court in Zion, Illinois. The verdict declared that the city seal (including a cross and the words "God Reigns") would have to be removed because it violated the separation of church and state. In June 1992, the Supreme Court refused to hear the case, so the city is now bound by law to remove this "offending" symbol from all of its municipal buildings, police cars, and so on. By some estimates 95 percent of the residents of Zion favor the present emblem. But the wishes of the people are irrelevant because the courts have overruled their preference. The person who chose to protest the seal in the first place has moved from the area.

Just think! The city of Zion could hold a contest to choose a new city seal. But if a design were submitted with a cross, even if 100 percent of the residents voted in favor of it, the seal would have to be discarded because it would be deemed unconstitutional.

The atheist who encouraged the resident to file the complaint is now going uninvited from community to community looking for other religious symbols that he insists must be removed from all public facilities—all in the name of the First Amendment.

In June 1992, the Supreme Court, based on a complaint from one student in Rhode Island, voted 5-4 that prayers in graduation ceremonies are unconstitutional. Once again the grievance of one person removed important freedoms from all public high schools, and possibly all public colleges and universities in the United States.

With the First Amendment turned on its head and interpreted in ways that the founding fathers would never have dreamed possible, freedom of speech is systematically being taken away in every area of public life. In Decatur, Illinois, a primary school teacher discovered the word *God* in a phonics textbook and ordered the seven-year-olds in her class to strike it out, saying that it is against the law to mention God in a public school.

In Virginia, a school principal requested that a handicapped girl stop bringing her Bible on the school bus. Reading the Bible on a vehicle being operated under the auspices of the state was deemed to be contrary to separation of church and state. After pressure from the Rutherford Institute, a body dedicated to the preservation of religious freedom, the principal backed down.

In Philadelphia, schoolchildren were asked to write a paper on the subject of "power." One girl received her teacher's approval to write on the power of God. But she was barred from presenting her paper publicly in class because other students might be "offended." Again, this intrusion of religion into the school supposedly violated the separation of church and state. The student who wrote on "The Power of Ghosts" read his paper in class. But a paper on the power of God had to be presented in the privacy of the teacher's office.

Where will this end? Several years ago my family had the privilege of visiting the People's Republic of China, a thoroughly Communist country that prides itself on the separation of church and state. Official government policy is that the church can operate in all areas that are not controlled by the government. When we pressed the issue of freedom, our tour guide finally said, "Of course we have freedom of religion. People are free to believe whatever they like *in their own minds.*"

In America although expansive rights are given to pornographers and artists who specialize in obscenity, others are told that they cannot utter the word *God* in a graduation address. I'm convinced that the enemies of religion will not be satisfied until God is expunged from every facet of American life and religion is confined to the human mind. Make no mistake, the militant secularists are determined that their vision for a godless America become a reality.

The Schools

Increasingly the curriculum in many public schools is becoming a primer in occultism. *Impressions,* a curriculum used in many school districts (about eighty districts in California alone), instructs teachers and students in how to cast spells. One teacher's manual reads, "Tell the children that a magician has cast a spell on some children. Have them work in pairs to write the magic spell the magician used. Have each pair write another spell to reverse the first spell. Have them chant their spells."

About 16,000 school districts use the *Pumsey the Dragon* curriculum, by Jill Anderson. Many of the relaxation techniques used are identical to those used in hypnosis. Another curriculum called *Duso the Dolphin* employs relaxation techniques and sends hypnotized youngsters off on guided fantasies to a place called Aquatron. Is it any wonder that many teachers order their pupils not to tell their parents about these kinds of classes?

Massive, federally subsidized, sex education programs entered the American public school system in the 1970s. As these courses have been imposed upon schoolchildren, pregnancies among teenagers have soared. The attempt has been made to strip away all normal reserve and protective inhibitions by giving explicit teaching on how to be immoral. Graphic movies, the pairing of boys and girls for explicit sexual discussion, and the teaching of homosexual values are standard fare.

Students are told that there is no yardstick by which moral actions can be judged; sexual behavior of all kinds is permissible. In one workbook students are encouraged to draw a picture of Mother and Father making love; then they are to discuss how they feel about the sex act. In some instances students watch a steamy sex film; then boys and girls pair off and each girl is required to roll a condom over her partner's finger. This is so-called "value free education!"

The November 21, 1992, edition of the *Chicago Tribune* had a article entitled "Teens Get 'Say Yes' to Sex Guide." About eight hundred students in a local high school were presented with an eighteen-page, slang-filled pamphlet entitled *Just Say Yes*. The information was distributed by a coalition that includes the radical homosexual groups ACT UP and Queer Nation. The manual, which comes complete with information on how to experience every sexual aberration, is, in the words of a spokesman, "pro-sex, pro-gay, pro-lesbian and pro-choice." Although this information was not sanctioned by the school and the administration was opposed to it, one can only wonder what would happen if a coalition of Christians were to hand out material giving reasons for abstinence before marriage. This would be decried as the work of fundamentalists bent on "imposing their morality" on impressionable youngsters!

Carol Everett, who managed two abortion clinics in the Dallas/Fort Worth area, said that these clinics depend on sex education in the schools. It works like this: Sex education encourages students to be immoral; and although information about contraceptives is given, it is a well-known fact that students will not regularly practice birth control; therefore, more sex education produces more pregnancies; more pregnancies produce more abortions; and more abortions produce more money for the clinics.

In a survey, one thousand sexually active teenaged girls were asked to name the topic on which they wanted more information. Eighty-four percent checked "How to say no without hurting the other person's feelings." Yet if a teacher wanted to conduct a class on how to say no, he or she would be told that this is not in keeping with "value free" education.

Abortion

About 1.5 million babies are aborted every year in the United States. These little ones are defenseless in the presence of the adults who put them to death.

According to Carol Everett, evidence is now beginning to surface that girls who have had an abortion have a greater tendency to abuse the children they decide to keep later on. Understandably, these young women are angry— angry at the men who impregnate them and then abandon them; angry at parents who often insist on an abortion for the sake of the family reputation; angry with the school system that taught them that it was acceptable to be immoral. Worse, they feel empty and guilty knowing they have killed their children.

What chance do the 400,000 teenaged girls who had an abortion last year have to grow up to be mothers who can communicate wholesome values to their children? And what about the millions of others who have had abortions in the past twenty years?

President Clinton has said that he supports "The Freedom of Choice Act," which if ratified by Congress would take abortion out of the hands of state legislators and even out of the hands of the Supreme Court. This bill permits no limits on the killing of unborn babies. As James Dobson has said, this bill would permit aborting a girl because the mother wants a boy; or it would permit an abortion for no reason at all until the day before delivery. This is called "a woman's right to choose."

The Media

Democratic Senator Robert Byrd of West Virginia has written an excellent critique of the television industry: "With each dose of vulgarity, profanity, pornography, promiscuity, assault, murder and other violence, we become less uncomfortable with those crimes and vices until at last our consciences lose the ability to object to them." He goes on to say that we should not be surprised to hear that teenagers murder their parents in cold blood. We should not be surprised that teenagers become drug users or alcoholics.

Television talk shows draw attention to the most deviant sexual aberrations and give the impression that such behavior is normal. As cable television and rental videos have invaded our homes, every standard of decency is violated.

It is estimated that 60 percent of all pornography falls into the hands of children. Considering that this is a multibillion dollar industry, there is simply no way to estimate the damaging effects this flood of impurity will have as it spills into our culture.

Homosexual Rights

As I write, New York City's new sex education curriculum for first graders has generated controversy. The material is designed to "challenge sexual myths" by defining a homosexual household as a normal family unit and propagating the myth that 10 percent of each class will grow up to be homosexual. It includes *Heather Has Two Mommies* and *Gloria Goes to Gay Pride* as supplemental materials. Over the objection of many parents, homosexual values will be imposed on their children—like it or not.

If you think that our churches are immune to the homosexual agenda, keep dreaming. According to the *Gay Blade*, a homosexual newspaper in Washington, with a liberal administration in place the targets will be Christian schools and churches. The goal is that no Christian organization will be able to dismiss an employee—even a pastor—because of homosexuality without breaking the law. The next step is that homosexuals be granted minority status and hence fall under affirmative action laws that would force churches and schools to hire them. Also, churches would be required to marry homosexual couples.

As I write, a shocking prohomosexual bill has been prepared and may soon be submitted to Congress. The bill S 574 and its House companion HR 1430, gives sodomy legal protection. The House version is sponsored by Barney Frank, whose male lover ran a prostitution ring out of Frank's house. This bill would give the same rights to lesbian and homosexual couples as are given to a husband and wife. Homosexuals will have the right to adopt children, and schools will be forced to teach that sodomy is as normal as heterosexuality. The implications for our schools, churches, and homes are far-reaching.

The lines are drawn. The cultural war continues. God has graciously given us the privilege of being His representatives in the midst of a society that is rapidly reaping the results of a militant secular agenda. Where do we go from here?

A HISTORICAL PERSPECTIVE

For 2,000 years the church has almost always existed under political regimes and cultures that were hostile to the Christian message. We immediately think of the persecutions that Christians endured throughout the Roman Empire during the early centuries of the church. Believers were not tortured because they believed in Jesus; in Rome one was free to believe in whatever god he wished. What galled the Romans was that Christians believed that *Christ was the only true God*. And because Christians were not willing to confess "Caesar is Lord" they were seen as politically subversive. Though some compromised their convictions, most stood for their faith. Countless thousands were put to death because they believed that some things were more important than blending in with the controlling ideas of their generation.

Some Christians reasoned that it would be advantageous if they had political power. Then they could use the sword to impose Christian beliefs on society as a whole. After Constantine became emperor in A.D. 312, Christianity became the official religion of the Roman Empire. Church and state were united; in fact, by the eighth century the state was under the authority of the church. When the pope crowned Charles the Great in Saint Peter's Basilica on Christmas day, A.D. 800, the authority of the church was uncontested.

As the church grew in power, its corruption increased. Its political, religious, and moral decay was so pervasive that many true believers tried to break away from the church's authority. For this they were persecuted—many were drowned or killed with the sword. The true church insisted that with the coming of Constantine nothing had changed. In the early centuries they were put to death by pagans; now they were put to death by official Christendom. Either way, *they were a minority who elicited hostility from the cultural, ecclesiastical, and political powers of their time.*

Why do we think it should be different for us? Must we think that the church can survive only in those countries that are tolerant of the Christian message? Even in our day, have we forgotten Russia, Romania, and China? The church survived in these countries without any political power at all. The consistent lesson of 2,000 years of church history is that *the church does not need freedom to be faithful.*

Read almost any of the epistles in the New Testament, and you will be reading a message to a church that was in the throes of some kind of persecution. Whether at Corinth, Philippi, Ephesus, or the scattered groups to whom 1 Peter was written—all of those believers were trying to be authentically Christian in a pagan culture. The author of the book of Hebrews chided his readers by comparing their suffering with that of Christ and the martyrs. He wrote, "You have not yet resisted to the point of shedding blood in your striving against sin" (Hebrews 12:4). He reminded them that, though they thought times were tough, they had not yet paid the ultimate price for faithfulness.

God is humbling the American church. In the early eighties we looked to the Moral Majority to halt our moral and spiritual toboggan slide. We thought our hope lay in the Congress, in the courts, in the White House. Evangelicals, we were told, held the balance of power. We could elect anyone we wanted, lobby for any laws we thought were right, and use the ballot box to tell the country that "we aren't going to take it anymore."

We should be thankful that the church has been awakened to the need to be involved in politics. But we must not be deluded—politics cannot save us. Politics is based on numbers, and numbers are based on coalitions that quickly fall apart when other issues become important. Actually, the Moral Majority never was a "majority."

Cal Thomas, who was vice president of the Moral Majority from 1980 to 1985, says that such an approach cannot work now because we are living in a post-Christian culture. The majority no longer accepts traditional, biblical values. He says, "To appeal to this majority with the language and values of the past is to invite rejection, even ridicule." Let us recall that Solzhenitsyn is quoted as saying to a friend that the scorn he received at Harvard (when he gave a speech on why it is necessary for America to turn back to God) hurt him more than his years in the Gulag. So much for America's respect for God and morality!

The day in which there was a "moral majority" is past (if indeed such a day ever existed). More recent polls suggest that only about 10 percent of Americans claim to have faith that affects the way they live. Let us admit that America's lost Christian heritage cannot be reclaimed through government. "As long as we are viewed as 'The Christian Right,'" says public policy expert Don Eberly, "the church will be seen as a peddler of ideology, rather than a force for renewal." And, as Charles Colson has observed, if we live by the political sword, we must die by it.

Let us also candidly admit that we must learn to be change-agents in a culture that is under judgment. God will not simply judge America in the future; already we see our nation paying a heavy price for its insistence that God can be summarily ignored. As we reap what we sow, all of us are affected.

The consequences of sin are always both immediate and long-term. The church is presently being disciplined for its sins; the more we buy into the world's values, the less impact we can have upon our culture. Someday there may be a cataclysmic reckoning, but we are paying for our sins right now.

When God told Israel that disobedience would have severe consequences, He ended by saying, "Your sons and your daughters shall be given to another people, while your eyes shall look on and yearn for them continually; but there shall be nothing you can do" (Deuteronomy 28:32). The severest judgment was the scattering of Israel's families.

Though in a different way, the same is happening in America today. One-half of all children born this year will live with only a single parent, and the statistics within the church are not much better. The emotional scars left on our children will be passed on to the next generation. Today sons are crying for their fathers; daughters are crying for their mothers. Wives are filled with rage, and men with hatred. The full effects of our disobedience will spill into an ever-widening flood in the next generation.

Should we collapse in despair, wring our hands, and give up? Shall we retreat from the world of politics, art, journalism, and education? Shall we sell our assets and go into hiding, waiting for the end of the world?

No, God has a job for us to do. He has not abandoned His people. This is a wonderful opportunity for the church to be the church. This is a time that calls for courage and commitment that is worthy of the God we serve.

What should we be doing at a time

when the barriers are crumbling and our families are breaking up? What should we be doing when millions of children are being aborted and hostile political forces are trying to impose a godless agenda on our schools and churches? What should we do when the courts circumvent democracy and insist that all of us march in step with a liberal agenda?

We must rethink our calling and refocus our objectives. We must cling to what is unmovable in an age when everything that has been nailed down is being torn up. We must be as faithful as those who have gone before us.

Where *do* we go from here?

FIVE UNSHAKABLE PILLARS

Pessimism is out of place in the presence of the promises of God. "We cannot," as the saying goes, "talk about standing on the Rock of Ages and then act as if we are clinging to our last piece of driftwood." Could our anxiety about the future reflect fear—the fear that we shall have to confess our own weaknesses and trust God in ways that are unfamiliar? Five unshakable pillars will provide a firm footing as we stand against our present cultural stream.

God Still Reigns

Sometimes God gives a leader to a nation who is *better* than that nation deserves. Josiah was a righteous king who tried to turn Judah back to God at a time when the nation had slid into rebellion and idolatry. "Josiah was eight years old when he became king, and he reigned for thirty-one years in Jerusalem. . . .And he did right in the sight of the Lord" (2 Kings 22:1–2). Under his leadership the Book of the Law was found and read. The Passover was reinstituted. He removed witchcraft and occultism from the land.

But the nation had fallen so far into rebellion that those reforms barely delayed the coming judgment. "However, the Lord did not turn from the fierceness of His great wrath with which His anger burned against Judah, because of all the provocations with which Manasseh had provoked Him" (2 Kings 23:26). The cultural currents of Manasseh were so powerful that Josiah and his reforms could not turn the nation back to God. Josiah was a better king than the nation deserved.

Sometimes a leader is *far worse* than the nation deserves. We would all agree that the people of the former Soviet Union did not deserve Stalin; the people of Germany did not deserve Hitler. During such times, God reveals the evil of the human heart for all to see. And even through wicked leaders He purifies His church and accomplishes His purposes.

Sometimes God gives a leader to a nation that it *does* deserve. In the days of the Judges the people of Israel clamored for a king so they could be like all the other nations. God had other plans. But when the godly prophet Samuel prayed about the situation, the Lord replied, "Listen to the voice of the people in regard to all that they say to you, for they have not rejected you, but they have rejected Me from being king over them" (1 Samuel 8:7). So God gave them exactly what they wanted, a king after their own liking. Saul was anointed as the first king of the nation, and, due to his disobedience, Israel suffered. Saul was a rather accurate reflection of the people themselves. He was exactly what the nation deserved.

Yet in each of these instances God was in control. He does not do what is evil, of course, nor are people programmed like a computer to do His will. People choose; they do what they like or what seems best at the moment. Yet, through secondary causes, they act under the providential hand of God. That is why Daniel could write that "the Most High is ruler over the realm of mankind, and bestows it on whom He wishes and sets over it the lowliest of men" (Daniel 4:17).

The actions of a king, court, or president will never thwart the plan of God. No matter what evil plans are hatched on earth, "He who sits in the heavens laughs, the Lord scoffs at them" (Psalm 2:4). Whether the leader is Nero, George Washington, or Saddam Hussein, "there is no authority except from God, and those which exist are established by God" (Romans 13:1).

America faces a growing crisis in moral and political leadership. Thankfully, there are still many who have not bowed before the gods of this age. But as the restraints are increasingly cast aside and people compromise important principles for the sake of expedience, we must remember—*God still reigns!*

Regardless of who our leaders are, we are to offer "prayers, petitions and thanksgivings. . . .for kings and all who are in authority" (1 Timothy 1:1–2).

We pray because God reigns!

The Church Is Still Precious

Put yourself in a time machine and go back to the first century, when the common people had no part in selecting their leaders. As a Christian you are harassed for your faith in accordance with government policy. You are shunned in the marketplace. Your children are ridiculed as they play or work in the fields. You are constantly faced with questions: what is essential to my faith; what is not? Some of your friends who are outspoken about their faith are executed. Others remain silent, keeping their faith to themselves. How are you to survive in a pagan culture? Your loyalty to Christ and loyalty to the state are in constant conflict.

To those who actually lived in such oppression, Peter, who himself eventually died for his faith, wrote, "But you are a chosen race, a royal priesthood, a holy nation, a people for God's own possession, that you may proclaim the excellencies of Him who has called you out of darkness into His marvelous light" (1 Peter 2:9).

What follows is detailed instruction on how God would have us live within a hostile culture. But before the church can *do*, it must *be*. If we are not holy, we cannot be salt and light to society. We dare not think that we can substitute politics for purity. Knowing who we are gives us the courage to live as we should. Our roots must be firmly planted in our unchangeable relationship with God before we are prepared to live in this changeable culture.

First, *we are a chosen race*. That is, we were chosen in Christ before the foundation of the world, and even then our names were written in heaven (Revelation 13:8). The knowledge that we are precious to God inspires us to live up to our calling.

Second, *we are a royal priesthood*. In the Old Testament era the high priest could go into the Holy of Holies only one day a year. Today, we who are believers actually live in the Holy of Holies, for Christ has brought us into God's presence and left us there. For this reason we need never think that God has abandoned His people. When confronted with a hostile culture, we can daily come before God to receive grace to help in time of need. *The greater the need, the greater the grace.*

Third, *we are a holy nation*—that is, we are set apart to God. We should be astonished if the world welcomed our moral and political agenda. Christ exposes the sins of the world, and darkness loves darkness. Did He not tell us that the world, which hated Him, would hate us?

Finally, *we are, above all, a people for God's own possession.* No matter what personal battles we may face, we are still number one on God's list of priorities. We are the objects of His attention; He is preparing us to eternally display His grace and wisdom (Ephesians 2:7).

Such a calling should not fill us with pride but with humility. We should consider it an honor to be identified with Christ. Special blessings come with duly earned persecution.

Our calling is to live out the reality of who we are with dignity, kindness, and convictions. If we confront the world in anger or needlessly antagonize, we have abandoned our calling. We are to model the character of Christ in a world that is skeptical, a world that is convinced that God doesn't matter.

As believers we can be sure that *there is no such thing as meaningless suffering*. After all, we are God's special possession.

Our Mission Is Still Clear

What should we be doing? Peter says that we are to "proclaim the excellencies of Him who has called us out of darkness into His marvelous light" (1 Peter 2:9). Remember, this was written to those who were targeted by the pagans for special harassment. Just as flowers sometimes do not emit their fragrance unless they are crushed, so believers often do not exude the beauty of Christ unless they feel the pressure of the world. No matter the political regime or the hostility of the culture, believers are to make Christ attractive to the world.

First, *we represent Christ by our lifestyles*. "Keep your behavior excellent among the Gentiles, so that in the thing in which they slander you as evil doers, they may on account of your good deeds, as they observe them, glorify God in the day of visitation" (1 Peter 2:12).

We are to continue doing good deeds no matter how intense the pressure becomes. If we, like the Pharisees, stand in judgment on our culture without an honest sense of our own failures, if we see the world as our enemy and act as though we have not contributed to our cultural drift, we lose credibility.

Why is the world so smug in its unbelief? It has lost faith in the believability of God. Most people have not seen a credible Christian witness, a model of what a person in whom God is alive and working is like. They have seen angry, judgmental Christians, they have seen inconsistent Christians, and they have seen scandals that have revealed some ministers to be obvious hypocrites. Is it any wonder that they dismiss our faith? Humanly speaking, there may be powerful reasons why the world does not believe.

Often we have not been adept at separating a sinner from his sins. Yes, we are opposed to imposing homosexual values on society, but we must deal compassionately with those who struggle with such a lifestyle and with those who have AIDS. Yes, we are opposed to divorce, but we must deal compassionately with those who have experienced the pain of marital failure. Yes, we are opposed to abortion; but to every woman who has terminated a human life, we affirm that Christ does forgive. The world needs to know that Christ died for sinners, even *great* sinners.

On every level the church must show itself as a redeemed community, filled with imperfect people who themselves struggle with all the failings of the world. The difference is that we have a new sense of identity as those who belong to God. We know both the reality of sin and the joy of grace. The excellencies of Christ are best revealed through the lives of those who are compassionate because they themselves are profoundly aware of their own shortcomings. Let us remember that what the world needs most is *to see Jesus*.

A mission agency that monitors the church in the People's Republic of China asked thousands of believers what drew them to faith in Christ. Many answers were given, but one was listed most often: the joy in the lives of believers with whom they came in contact made them envious.

Evangelism must be our priority, but our message must be authenticated by changed lives. We must learn to serve as Christ did. We must be models of love and humility in this day of egoism and crass selfishness. People are skeptical of words. Today's generation says, "Show me and I will believe. Show me that you care."

Second, *we must win the intellectual and moral war through loving confrontation and persuasiveness.* Peter wrote, "Sanctify Christ as Lord in your hearts, always being ready to make a defense to every one who asks you to give an account for the hope that is in you, yet with gentleness and reverence" (1 Peter 3:15).

Apologetics, the defense of the faith, must change its focus. Twenty years ago apologetics was a study that showed the superiority of Christianity over other religions. Today apologetics must be taught as a coherent defense of the Christian worldview in opposition to a smorgasbord of contradictory and even absurd ideas. We must be able to discuss all aspects of Christianity in a reasonable, believable way.

All of the evidence is on our side

in the war of ideas that rages in America today. We have excellent reasons to believe that Christ is superior to all of the other religious leaders of the world. As for abortion, even the world has to admit that a fetus is actually a baby. (Only this can explain why mothers of cocaine babies are being charged with delivery of drugs to a minor.) In the debate about values we can prove that without a belief in God there can be no morality whatever. Every believer must be trained to "give a reason for the hope within him."

Third, *we must do all we can to strengthen our families.* The future stability of America is dependent upon a commitment to marriage and the teaching of children. Many parents are removing their children from the public school system because they have discovered that their school cannot be changed. Home schools and private schools will have to absorb millions of children if we are serious about preserving Christian values. Other parents are working actively on school boards and in their PTAs, trying to make their schools what they should be. These are the kinds of decisions and sacrifices parents will have to make in this pagan culture.

Christians must stand for truth wherever God has planted them. We have been intimidated because of the caricatures of the press. We have been pictured as uneducated, puritanical, opinionated, and one-dimensional. In short, we are *kooks*. These distortions have caused us to withdraw, lick our wounds, and adopt an unhealthy persecution complex.

Os Guinness has warned that when we begin to feel sorry for ourselves we must remember "that the effect of playing the victim is to reject the ethic of Christ and resort to a politics of resentment. The politics of resentment is the politics of revenge." We are not a majority, but God keep us from becoming an angry, vindictive minority! Self-pity loses sight of the promises of God and leads to a mind-set of withdrawal, an attitude that says, "Since they hate us, let them rot." How unlike our Master!

Evangelicals must penetrate the world of television, law, journalism, and government. More than ever, we need the impact of every Christian. We might complain that America is being stolen, but it may be more accurate to say that

Christians are *giving* it away. If America will ever reclaim its heritage, it will not be because powerful men will lead political crusades; it will not be because we have learned how to out-vote our opponents.

In a letter to the supporters of Prison Fellowship, Charles Colson says we will win only by building up the body of Christ: "Our place is on our knees, in the streets helping people in need, winning our neighbors and colleagues to a Christian world view by speaking the truth in love. We will win the cultural war one house, one block at a time, as God's people are trained and equipped by the church and then go out and live their faith in the world."

The day of the casual Christian is over. No longer is it possible to drift along, hoping that no tough choices will have to be made. At this point in American history, any moral and spiritual progress will have to be won at great cost. The darker the night, the more important every candle becomes.

Our Focus Is Still Heaven

Years ago we heard the cliche "Some people are so heavenly minded that they are no earthly good." My observation is that this no longer applies today. Most of us are so earthly minded that we are no heavenly good! The pressures of life have inspired us to borrow the values of the world.

Peter writes, "Beloved, I urge you as aliens and strangers to abstain from fleshly lusts, which wage war against the soul" (1 Peter 2:11). Strangers and aliens understand their present surroundings and know where they are headed.

First, *we must see this world as temporary.* Many of us are not meaningfully involved in our political and moral battles until we ourselves are affected. As Francis Schaeffer told us a decade ago, the primary desire of most American Christians is "to live in personal peace and affluence." If we are not on the front lines, we may become indifferent to others who are engulfed in the cultural battles that erupt around us.

When we see our future in this world threatened by paganism, we will soon discover the extent to which we love this passing world. The apostle Paul taught that the real world was eternal, unchanging, and unseen. Pilgrims who pass through territory en route to their permanent home do not drive in their stakes too deeply. They know they are leaving in the morning.

Second, *we need to redefine what separation from the world means.* The church is to be in the world as a ship is in the ocean. But when the ocean gets into the ship, there is trouble. For decades the evangelical ship has been taking on water. It is difficult for us to rescue others when we ourselves are being drawn under. No longer dare we embrace the world's entertainment and values. It is time for commitment, a time for repentance.

We can expect that the distinction between the world and the church will become more clearly defined as spiritual darkness settles on the land. When we visited China, we were told that persecution wiped out all theological liberalism. Understandably so, for why would anyone be willing to die for a Christ who was a mere man?

America isn't there yet, of course. But the principle still stands: *When being a Christian is no longer popular, there is a clearer distinction between the church and the world.* We then begin to distinguish between those who really love

Christ and those who joined the evangelical bandwagon for the ride.

Never before in American history has it been so important to become an active part of a network of other believers for worship, encouragement, instruction, and prayer. Bible studies, prayer groups, and discipleship training must have as their goal the training of believers to be change-agents in their world.

We should not think it strange when we hear that the secular press is biased against the Christian faith. We should not think it strange when the police arrest Christians who are using a public park for prayer. We should not think it strange when the ACLU, with its strict stand against the intrusion of religion in schools, nevertheless is willing to defend the right of a high school to show *The Last Temptation of Christ.*

We think these things are strange because we have forgotten that such treatment should be expected as part of our calling. To quote Peter once more:

> Beloved, do not be surprised at the fiery ordeal among you, which comes upon you for your testing,

> as though some strange thing were happening to you; but to the degree that you share the sufferings of Christ, keep on rejoicing; so that also at the revelation of His glory, you may rejoice with exultation. If you are reviled for the name of Christ, you are blessed, because the spirit of glory and of God rests upon you. By no means let any of you suffer as a murderer, or thief, or evildoer, or a troublesome meddler; but if anyone suffers as a Christian, let him not feel ashamed, but in that name let him glorify God. (1 Peter 4:12–16)

Clearly, not all suffering that Christians endure brings glory to God; not all of it is worthy of the name. Much suffering is brought upon us because of our own actions. Only the suffering that comes to us because of our clear commitment to Christ receives special reward. Such suffering is precious to the Almighty.

What should the world see when we are called upon to suffer? How should a Christian professor react when he is fired for refusing to favor gay rights? How shall we react if the day comes when churches are sued for not hiring homosexuals or refusing to ordain women? How should a Christian student respond when he is told that witnessing for Christ is contrary to the university's politically correct view that all religions are of equal value?

Yes, we must choose to fight, but let us do it with love, integrity, and a witness for the saving grace of Christ. We must never fight fire with fire, acting like the world, when in point of fact we are citizens of another country. Let us make sure that our fighting is done on our knees and with wet eyes.

The best example of how to handle persecution comes from the first-century Christians who had their property confiscated and then were thrown into jail for their faith. How did they react? "For you...accepted joyfully the seizure of your property, knowing that you have for yourselves a better possession and an abiding one" (Hebrews 10:34). They accepted the seizure of their property and even imprisonment with joy because they knew where their real home and future lay. They knew the meaning of the words *aliens* and *strangers*.

True pilgrims know that the battle is spiritual and not simply political or even moral. Satan is not more powerful today than he was in the past. He is, however, more visible, especially when the church retreats from meaningful engagement with the world. Satan is especially visible when the church acts on its own initiative without active faith in God.

Our Victory Is Still Certain

Will America turn back to a belief in biblical absolutes? Will the freedom of speech return to our classrooms? Will the holocaust in our abortion clinics end? We simply do not know the answer. God may graciously intervene and send this nation to its knees. G.K. Chesterton said, "At least five times the Faith has to all appearances gone to the dogs. In each of these five cases, it was the dog that died."

On the other hand, America may continue to self-destruct, headed for moral oblivion. Whether or not we win this cultural war is really up to God; whether we are faithful is, to a large extent, up to us.

We do not have to be victorious in this world to triumph in the next. We do not accept the world's philosophy that we have to have it all now or we will never have another chance. We do not have to seek retaliation for all the personal injustices we might experience in this life. *We believe in another world.*

During the terrible Boxer Rebellion in China at the turn of this century (the leaders were so nicknamed because they practiced gymnastics and calisthenics), the "boxers" captured a mission station, then placed a flat cross on the ground. They gave instruction that those who trampled the cross as they came out of the building would be set free; those who walked around the cross would be executed. The first seven students trampled the cross under their feet and were released. But the eighth student, a young girl, knelt beside the cross and prayed for strength. Then she slowly walked around the cross to face the firing squad. Strengthened by her example, every one of the more than ninety other students followed her to death. Did they win?

Throughout history during times of oppression the sole cry of believers has almost always been to God. Without spite, revenge, and hostility, they, like their Master, believed that they were called to pay the ultimate price. Often they remained calm and forgiving.

Losers? Yes, from the standpoint of this world. But they belonged to another world where they were winners indeed. Christ Himself appeared to be a loser if we look only at the cross and fail to see the resurrection and ascension. We dare not judge success by months, days, or years, but by eternity. In the end every tongue will give God glory, "that at the name of Jesus every knee should bow, of those who are in heaven, and on earth, and under the earth, and that every tongue should confess that Jesus Christ is Lord, to the glory of God the Father" (Philippians 2:10–11).

"It is better to fail at a cause that will ultimately succeed than to succeed in a cause that will ultimately fail," wrote Peter Marshall. Better to be faithful in building the church than to succeed at something that doesn't really matter.

After a young African was martyred for his faith, this writing was found in his room:

I'm part of the fellowship of the unashamed, the die has been cast, I have stepped over the line, the decision has been made—I'm a disciple of Jesus Christ—I won't look back, let up, slow down, back away or be still.

My past is redeemed, my present makes sense, my future is secure—I'm finished and done with low living, sight walking, smooth knees, colorless dreams, tamed visions, worldly talking, cheap giving and dwarfed goals.

My face is set, my gait is fast, my goal is heaven, my road is narrow, my way is rough, my companions are few, my guide is reliable, my mission is clear. I won't give up, shut up, let up until I have stayed up, stored up, prayed up for the cause of Jesus Christ.

I must go till He comes, give till I drop, preach till everyone knows, work till He stops me and when He comes for His own, He will have no trouble recognizing me because my banner will have been clear.

With this kind of resolve we will,

with God's help, have the strength to survive against our cultural stream, or perhaps even reverse it. Of course, we are a minority, but armed with the promises of God we can have a spiritual impact that is greater than our numbers might suggest.

It may come down to a simple question: *Are we willing to pay the price?*

Other booklets by Erwin W. Lutzer:

Coming to Grips with Heaven
Coming to Grips with Hell
Coming to Grips with Death and Dying
Coming to Grips with God's Discipline of the Believer
Coming to Grips with Unanswered prayer
Coming to Grips with Satan's Plan for Your life
Coming to Grips with Your Role in the Workplace
Coming to Grips with Your Sexual Past
Coming to Grips with Marital Conflict
Coming to Grips with Homosexuality
Coming to Grips with the Antichrist's New Age Roots
Coming to Grips with the Role of Europe in Prophecy

Moody Press, a ministry of the Moody Bible Institute, is designed for education, evangelization, and edification. If we may assist you in knowing more about Christ and the Christian life, please write us without obligation: Moody Press, c/o MLM, Chicago, Illinois 60610.